AI IN AUTOMOTIVE INDUSTRY
AI-Powered Innovation in Cars, Supply Chains, and Smart Mobility
by **Sayeed Siddiqui**

Copyright Page

First Edition: 2025
ISBN: (assigned)
Published by: Amazon KDP

Dedication

To the innovators, engineers, and
visionaries who dared to dream of a
self-driving future — and to those who make
it safer, smarter, and more sustainable
every day.

Table of Contents

Chapter 1: Introduction — A New Era for Mobility

The world is shifting gears—and AI is in the driver's seat.

The automotive industry stands on the threshold of a revolution—one not merely of hardware or horsepower, but of intelligence. From mechanical marvels to digitized ecosystems, the way we design, build, buy, and use vehicles is being reshaped by a force as powerful as the steam engine once was: Artificial Intelligence (AI).

AI is not just a tool; it is the transformative engine behind the new era of mobility. It's turning cars into co-pilots, production lines into predictive platforms, and transportation systems into self-optimizing networks. This chapter introduces the scope, urgency, and unprecedented promise of AI in the automotive world—laying the foundation for everything that follows in this guidebook.

The Transformation of a Century-Old Industry

Since Karl Benz unveiled the Motorwagen in 1885, the automotive industry has seen numerous innovations—combustion engines, mass production, fuel injection, GPS, hybrid drivetrains. But these milestones pale in comparison to the scale of transformation brought on by AI. Why? Because AI doesn't just improve a process—it redefines it.

Historically, innovation in this sector followed a linear trajectory: faster engines, safer frames, better fuel efficiency. But AI introduces exponential potential. A car no longer just takes you from point A to B—it learns, adapts, predicts, and interacts. It can detect an obstacle in milliseconds, optimize your route based on real-time traffic, or alert the mechanic before a fault becomes critical. The vehicle is becoming a living, thinking entity on wheels.

What's Driving the Shift?

Several overlapping forces are making AI indispensable in automotive:

1. **Data Explosion**: Every modern vehicle contains sensors that generate gigabytes of data per hour—from engine diagnostics to lane markings, pedestrian movement to tire pressure. AI is essential to process and make real-time decisions from this data flood.

2. **Demand for Autonomy**: With ride-sharing platforms and urban congestion, consumers are seeking alternatives to traditional driving. AI enables autonomous driving that promises safer, more efficient, and less stressful transportation.

3. **Connected Infrastructure**: Smart cities are integrating vehicle-to-everything (V2X) communication—traffic lights, roads, weather systems, and even other cars talking to each other. AI

orchestrates this web of interactions.

4. **Sustainability Goals**: Governments and consumers are pushing for cleaner, greener vehicles. AI optimizes electric battery use, predicts optimal charging times, and reduces emissions through intelligent driving behaviors.

5. **Digital Expectations**: We live in the era of smart homes, smart phones, and smart assistants. Consumers now expect their vehicles to provide intelligent, personalized experiences—from climate control to entertainment.

Defining AI in the Automotive Context

In layman's terms, AI refers to machines mimicking human-like capabilities—reasoning, learning, problem-solving. In automotive, it translates to:

- **Computer Vision**: Cameras and sensors enabling object detection (pedestrians, signs, lanes).

- **Natural Language Processing (NLP)**: Voice-controlled assistants that understand human speech.

- **Machine Learning (ML)**: Algorithms that improve driving performance based on past data.

- **Reinforcement Learning**: Systems that self-improve through trial and error.

- **Neural Networks**: Mimicking human brain processing to support advanced decision-making.

These AI components are often combined with other technologies—like high-definition mapping, radar/LiDAR, cloud computing, and edge devices—to create robust driving intelligence.

Four Levels of AI Integration

The impact of AI spans four major layers of the automotive lifecycle:

1. **AI in Product Development:**

   o Accelerates design via generative algorithms.

   o Simulates crash impacts and stress testing virtually.

   o Enhances ergonomics using biometric modeling.

2. **AI in Manufacturing:**

   o Robotics systems with vision-enabled accuracy.

   o Predictive analytics to reduce downtime.

   o Digital twins for real-time factory performance replication.

3. **AI in In-Vehicle Systems:**

- Driver monitoring for fatigue or distraction.

- Real-time adaptation of infotainment, temperature, seat settings.

- Navigation that learns user habits and weather patterns.

4. **AI in After-Sales Services**:

- AI chatbots for customer service.

- Predictive maintenance alerts.

- Usage-based insurance pricing.

Case Study: Tesla's AI-First Model

Tesla's approach to AI is holistic. Its vehicles are embedded with a Full Self-Driving (FSD) computer that processes inputs from eight cameras, ultrasonic sensors, and a radar system. What makes Tesla unique is its **fleet learning** capability. Every Tesla on the road sends back anonymized data that helps improve the neural network—whether it's about potholes, traffic behavior, or rare scenarios like a pedestrian with an umbrella crossing at an angle.

Tesla also runs a Dojo supercomputer to train AI models on billions of video frames. With regular over-the-air software updates, a Tesla bought today could drive significantly better a year later—without any hardware change. This software-centric, AI-driven model has reshaped what consumers expect from an automaker.

Not Just Tesla: Global Pioneers

The AI race is truly global:

- **Germany**: BMW and Audi use AI to create "digital twins" of manufacturing plants, simulate vehicle aerodynamics, and develop smart assistants.

- **USA**: Ford's BlueCruise, GM's Super Cruise, and Waymo's autonomous taxis all utilize AI for navigation, decision-making, and safety.

- **China**: XPeng and Baidu Apollo are embedding AI for driverless navigation and voice-controlled personalization.

- **India**: Tata Elxsi and Mahindra are using AI for telematics, warranty analytics, and adaptive cruise systems.

These efforts go far beyond marketing gimmicks—they're part of a global shift to reimagine what a car is and how it behaves.

Opportunities Unleashed

AI is unlocking a wave of opportunities across the automotive ecosystem:

- **Startups** are developing niche innovations—sensor fusion algorithms, AI chips for edge devices, fleet intelligence platforms.

- **Tier-1 Suppliers** (like Bosch, Continental) are building AI-powered modules for OEMs.

- **Dealerships** are leveraging AI for dynamic pricing, customer profiling, and virtual test drives.

- **Logistics and Fleet Managers** are adopting AI for fuel optimization, asset tracking, and driver behavior analysis.

AI isn't replacing automotive professionals—it's **amplifying their capabilities**. Designers become innovators, mechanics become data interpreters, and drivers become co-pilots.

Challenges Ahead

As with any emerging technology, there are significant roadblocks:

1. **Regulatory Hurdles**: No global standard exists for AI-driven driving. Legal frameworks lag behind innovation.

2. **Ethical Dilemmas**: Should an AV prioritize passenger safety over pedestrians in an unavoidable crash?

3. **Cybersecurity Threats**: Connected vehicles are potential targets for hacking. Securing AI systems is paramount.

4. **Public Trust**: Accidents involving AI—even if statistically rare—generate disproportionate backlash.

5. **Cost and Infrastructure**: High-performance chips, LiDAR sensors, and 5G integration remain expensive.

Without addressing these hurdles, the AI-driven future may stall before it truly begins.

Thought Experiment: The 2035 Scenario

Imagine a weekday morning in 2035:

You summon your car via voice command. It knows your schedule, pre-loads your playlist, and selects the fastest route avoiding construction. As you recline, your vehicle communicates with city infrastructure to sail through green lights and reduce emissions by coordinating with other traffic.

Midway, it reroutes you due to a weather-based hazard, informing your workplace assistant about a two-minute delay. Upon arrival, it drops you off and autonomously heads to a charging dock or earns money on a shared ride route.

This is not fiction. It's a logical outcome of current AI trajectories.

AI and Human Identity: The Philosophical Shift

AI is not just transforming mobility—it's challenging our relationship with cars. For over a century, driving has symbolized freedom, control, and identity. With AI, we're gradually shifting from **drivers to passengers**, from **controllers to collaborators**.

This philosophical shift mirrors other AI transformations—from doctors aided by diagnostic AI, to artists remixing with machine learning. The automotive industry becomes a reflection of our evolving place in the intelligent age.

Summary and Outlook

The automotive industry, once defined by combustion and chrome, is now defined by code and cognition. AI is enabling cars to see, learn, think, and act. It is connecting components that were once isolated—human emotion, urban planning, environmental science, and digital systems—into one harmonized flow.

The road ahead is filled with possibilities and pitfalls. But one thing is clear: those who harness AI's full potential will not just lead the market—they will **redefine the nature of motion** itself.

In the following chapters, we will explore these dimensions in depth—from design to manufacturing, autonomy to ethics—providing a full roadmap for professionals, entrepreneurs, and dreamers steering through the revolution.

Buckle up—the age of intelligent mobility has begun.

Chapter 2: Evolution of Automotive Technology

From horse-drawn carriages to intelligent electric fleets—the journey of automotive innovation is a mirror of human progress.

The automobile is not merely a means of transport—it's a symbol of civilization's ingenuity. Since its inception, the automobile has undergone radical transformations that reflect broader technological, social, and economic revolutions. Understanding how we arrived at today's AI-powered smart mobility solutions requires us to revisit the key milestones in the evolution of automotive technology.

This chapter explores the historic roots of automotive engineering, the mechanical revolutions that followed, the integration of electronics and software, and finally, the emergence of AI as a defining force. We also investigate how changing social behavior and environmental concerns have shaped innovation over time.

The Birth of Mobility: Mechanical Marvels and First Movers

The journey of the automobile began in the late 19th century. Though steam-powered vehicles appeared as early as the 1700s, it was **Karl Benz** who, in 1885, unveiled the first gasoline-powered car—the Benz Patent-Motorwagen. This three-wheeled contraption had a 0.75-horsepower engine and a maximum speed of 16 km/h. It marked the dawn of individual mechanized transportation.

Other inventors soon followed. **Gottlieb Daimler** and **Wilhelm Maybach** created a four-wheeled vehicle in 1886. By 1908, **Henry Ford's Model T** brought the concept of affordable, mass-produced vehicles to the common man through the revolutionary moving assembly line.

Key features of this era included:

- Manual ignition and crank starters.

- Wooden wheels and leaf spring suspension.

- No real safety features.

- Extremely limited reliability.

These early cars were luxuries, but they laid the foundation for mass personal mobility.

The Assembly Line Revolution: Scaling the Industry

Henry Ford's introduction of the **assembly line** in 1913 reduced the time to build a car from 12 hours to 90 minutes. This breakthrough:

- Dramatically lowered vehicle costs.

- Enabled scale manufacturing.

- Created jobs and urban centers centered around automotive production.

The success of Ford's model spurred global competition. By the 1920s and 30s, brands like **Chevrolet**, **Chrysler**, and **Volkswagen** emerged, focusing on incremental improvements in comfort and performance.

Technological advancements included:

- Pressed steel bodies for durability.

- Electrical systems with lights and starters.

- Hydraulic brakes.

- Basic dashboards and analog gauges.

The internal combustion engine became the industry standard, and a thriving network of mechanics, fuel stations, and dealerships followed.

The Post-War Boom and Birth of Modern Engineering

After World War II, the automotive industry entered a golden age:

- **Fuel injection systems** replaced carburetors.

- **Automatic transmissions** became common.

- **Radial tires**, **power steering**, and **air conditioning** enhanced user comfort.

By the 1960s and 70s, vehicles became cultural icons—from the Mustang to the Mini Cooper. But along with popularity came growing pains:

- Air pollution from leaded gasoline.

- Traffic fatalities from high-speed collisions.

- Oil dependency became a geopolitical issue.

Governments began enacting regulations for **emissions**, **safety standards**, and **fuel efficiency**. The **Environmental Protection Agency (EPA)** in the U.S. and similar institutions globally began pushing automakers toward cleaner technologies.

The Digital Shift: From Analog to Electronic Control Units

In the 1980s, a quiet revolution began—**digitization** of the automobile. Vehicles started incorporating:

- **Microcontrollers** and **sensors**.

- **Electronic Control Units (ECUs)** for fuel injection and ignition timing.

- **Anti-lock Braking Systems (ABS)**.

- **On-board diagnostics (OBD)**.

This marked the move from pure mechanical systems to **cyber-physical systems**. The vehicle was no longer a machine—it was becoming a computer on wheels.

By the 1990s and early 2000s:

- **Navigation systems** using GPS appeared.

- **Electronic Stability Control (ESC)** reduced crash risk.

- **Drive-by-wire systems** replaced mechanical linkages.

- **CAN Bus (Controller Area Network)** allowed ECUs to communicate.

Cars became more reliable, safer, and smarter. But this also created a new dependency: **software**.

The Software Age: Infotainment, Telematics, and Beyond

As computing costs dropped and mobile internet became ubiquitous, software began defining the driving experience:

- **Infotainment systems** brought touchscreens, voice control, and Bluetooth.

- **Vehicle Telematics** enabled real-time location tracking and remote diagnostics.

- **Connected Services** such as stolen vehicle tracking, concierge services, and live traffic alerts emerged.

The rise of **smartphones** influenced UI/UX expectations. People began expecting:

- Smartphone mirroring (Apple CarPlay, Android Auto).

- Over-the-air updates.

- Customizable dashboards and themes.

This phase set the stage for AI. With massive data collection and real-time connectivity, cars now had the necessary inputs to fuel intelligent behavior.

Electrification: The New Powertrain Paradigm

In parallel with digital advances, environmental concerns triggered the **electric vehicle (EV)** revolution. While EVs date back to the 1800s, only in the 2010s did they become commercially viable:

- **Tesla's Roadster** and **Model S** showed EVs could be fast, sexy, and smart.

- **Nissan Leaf** and **Chevy Bolt** provided affordability.

- **Government incentives**, carbon taxes, and emission bans accelerated adoption.

Electric vehicles differ fundamentally:

- Fewer moving parts.

- Instant torque and regenerative braking.

- High-voltage batteries and power electronics.

AI is critical in this domain for **battery management**, **range prediction**, **thermal optimization**, and **autonomous control**.

Safety First: The Rise of Advanced Driver-Assistance Systems (ADAS)

Arguably the most consumer-visible application of AI is in **ADAS**. These include:

- **Adaptive Cruise Control (ACC)**.

- **Lane Keeping Assist (LKA)**.

- **Traffic Sign Recognition**.

- **Blind Spot Monitoring**.

- **Forward Collision Warning (FCW)** and **Autonomous Emergency Braking (AEB)**.

These systems rely on:

- **Radar** and **ultrasound** for object detection.

- **Cameras** for visual perception.

- **Sensor fusion algorithms** to interpret scenarios.

AI models process millions of inputs per second to aid in decision-making. The result? A measurable decline in crash fatalities in vehicles equipped with ADAS.

The Autonomous Frontier: Self-Driving Vehicles

The holy grail of automotive AI is autonomy. The **SAE (Society of Automotive Engineers)** defines six levels of autonomy:

- **Level 0**: No automation.

- **Level 1–2**: Driver assistance (adaptive cruise, lane centering).

- **Level 3**: Conditional automation (hands-off, but alert).

- **Level 4**: High automation (no driver needed in geofenced areas).

- **Level 5**: Full automation under all conditions.

Companies leading the charge:

- **Waymo**: Robotaxi trials in Arizona.

- **Cruise (GM)**: Urban AV fleets in San Francisco.

- **Baidu Apollo**: Autonomous buses in China.

- **Nuro**: Driverless delivery pods.

Self-driving cars use:

- **Sensor arrays** (LiDAR, radar, ultrasonic).

- **Perception stacks** for 3D scene reconstruction.

- **Path planning algorithms** for safe navigation.

- **Reinforcement learning** to improve behavior over time.

Human-Machine Interface (HMI): The Digital Cockpit

AI is transforming how drivers interact with their vehicles:

- **Voice Assistants** like Alexa Auto and Cerence.

- **Gesture Controls** to open sunroofs or control music.

- **AR Windshields** for navigation and hazard alerts.

- **Biometric Access** using face or fingerprint recognition.

The cockpit is evolving from analog dials to **personalized, immersive environments**. Future vehicles may even adapt climate or lighting based on mood recognition.

Supply Chain Disruption and Digital Twins

Modern vehicles rely on global supply chains with thousands of components. AI helps in:

- **Predicting part shortages**.

- **Optimizing inventory** using demand sensing.

- **Simulating logistics routes** to avoid delays.

- **Creating digital twins** of factories for proactive monitoring.

Events like the **COVID-19 pandemic** and **semiconductor shortages** revealed the fragility of traditional models. AI-based resilience planning is now a competitive advantage.

Sustainability, Circular Economy, and AI

As automotive giants commit to **net-zero targets**, AI plays a role in:

- **Life cycle analysis (LCA)** of materials.

- **Predictive maintenance** to extend component life.

- **Optimizing recycling pathways** for batteries and parts.

- **Eco-routing** and smart charging for fleet efficiency.

AI is the glue holding together **greener manufacturing**, **intelligent logistics**, and **eco-conscious consumer services**.

Conclusion: From Mechanical to Cognitive Machines

The evolution of automotive technology is a story of constant reinvention. We began with steam and gasoline, moved through steel and silicon, and now enter an age of sensors and software. AI is not a layer—it is the new operating system of mobility.

This chapter traced the key transitions that brought us to today's intelligent vehicles. Understanding this historical context is vital to appreciate the next chapters, where we dive into AI's specific applications—from designing vehicles to creating entirely autonomous ecosystems.

Chapter 3: Autonomous Vehicles and Machine Learning

The dream of self-driving cars is no longer science fiction. Thanks to machine learning, it's fast becoming science fact.

Few innovations have captured the imagination of both engineers and the public like autonomous vehicles (AVs). From sci-fi depictions of sentient cars to today's pilotless taxi services in real cities, the notion of a vehicle driving itself safely and efficiently has moved from fantasy to feasibility.

But what powers this seemingly magical transformation? At the heart of autonomy is **machine learning (ML)**—a subset of artificial intelligence that enables vehicles to learn from data, adapt to environments, and make real-time decisions with human-like precision.

In this chapter, we dive into how autonomous vehicles work, the role of machine learning in enabling autonomy, the key technologies involved, the challenges and breakthroughs, and how this evolving field is changing the way we think about driving, ownership, and transportation itself.

The Vision: A World Without Drivers?

The appeal of autonomous vehicles is multifaceted:

- **Safety**: Over 90% of road accidents are due to human error—fatigue, distraction, intoxication, or poor judgment. AVs could eliminate much of this.

- **Accessibility**: Elderly, disabled, and non-drivers could enjoy newfound mobility.

- **Efficiency**: AI can optimize traffic flow, reduce congestion, and minimize fuel waste.

- **Convenience**: Passengers could work, rest, or be entertained during commutes.

- **Environmental Impact**: Fleet-based AVs can be optimized for lower emissions.

Companies from Silicon Valley to Stuttgart are investing billions into achieving this vision. But behind the clean lines of a prototype car is a labyrinth of machine learning models, simulations, data sets, and ethical quandaries.

Understanding Autonomy: The SAE Levels

The **Society of Automotive Engineers (SAE)** defines six levels of autonomy:

- **Level 0**: No automation. The driver does everything.

- **Level 1**: Driver assistance (e.g., adaptive cruise control).

- **Level 2**: Partial automation (e.g., lane-keeping + braking). Human monitors.

- **Level 3**: Conditional automation. The car drives, but the driver must intervene if needed.

- **Level 4**: High automation. No driver needed in certain conditions or locations.

- **Level 5**: Full automation under all conditions, no human control required.

As of 2025, most commercial vehicles are at Level 2. Experimental AVs like Waymo's are nearing Level 4 in geofenced areas.

Core Components of an Autonomous Vehicle

Autonomous driving is not a single technology—it's a **stack** of interrelated systems:

1. **Perception**: Understanding the environment through cameras, radar, LiDAR, and ultrasonic sensors.

2. **Localization**: Determining the vehicle's position within a map using GPS, IMU (Inertial Measurement Units), and SLAM (Simultaneous Localization and Mapping).

3. **Prediction**: Anticipating the behavior of pedestrians, cyclists, and other vehicles.

4. **Planning**: Creating a safe, efficient route and maneuver plan.

5. **Control**: Executing acceleration, braking, and steering actions.

6. **Decision-Making**: Choosing between multiple actions based on

context and learned experience.

Each of these modules relies heavily on **machine learning models** trained on vast amounts of driving data.

Machine Learning: The Brain Behind the Wheel

Machine Learning allows AVs to learn from examples rather than explicit programming. Types of ML used in autonomous vehicles include:

- **Supervised Learning**: Teaching a model using labeled data (e.g., "this is a stop sign").

- **Unsupervised Learning**: Clustering or detecting patterns without labels (e.g., anomaly detection in sensor data).

- **Reinforcement Learning**: Learning through trial and error, maximizing rewards over time.

- **Deep Learning**: Using neural networks to extract features and recognize complex patterns (e.g., facial recognition, pedestrian detection).

These models are applied to:

- **Object detection and classification** (cars, people, signs).

- **Trajectory prediction** for moving objects.

- **Behavioral cloning** (mimicking human driving behavior).

- **Semantic segmentation** of the driving scene.

- **Sensor fusion** (combining inputs for a complete view).

ML models are continuously updated through real-world driving data—creating a **feedback loop of learning**.

Case Study: Waymo

Waymo, a subsidiary of Alphabet (Google's parent), is a pioneer in AV development. It has logged over **20 million miles** of autonomous driving on public roads.

Key features:

- Uses a **custom sensor suite** including 360-degree LiDAR.

- Relies on **high-definition maps** accurate to centimeters.

- Employs **deep learning** for pedestrian behavior prediction.

- Integrates **reinforcement learning** for decision-making at intersections.

Waymo's vehicles operate in Phoenix, Arizona, as part of a commercial robotaxi service. The success has proven that AVs can function safely without human drivers—in controlled environments.

Data is the New Fuel

AVs require **massive datasets** to learn:

- 3D maps of cities.

- Traffic scenarios and edge cases.

- Annotated video for object recognition.

- Sensor readings under different weather conditions.

To improve safety and generalization, companies use:

- **Simulation environments** like CARLA and NVIDIA DriveSim to generate synthetic data.

- **Fleet learning** (e.g., Tesla's approach) where real-world data from every car improves the entire network.

- **Shadow mode testing**—running AI in parallel with human drivers to compare decisions without taking control.

This is an **endless learning cycle**. The more an AV drives, the smarter it becomes.

The Sensor Debate: LiDAR vs. Vision

A key debate in AV design is whether LiDAR (Light Detection and Ranging) is essential.

- **LiDAR advocates** (e.g., Waymo, Aurora) argue it provides accurate 3D depth maps, independent of lighting.

- **Vision-first companies** (e.g., Tesla) argue that AI-powered camera systems are cheaper, scalable, and closer to how humans drive.

Each approach has trade-offs:

- **LiDAR** is precise but expensive and sensitive to weather.

- **Cameras** are cheaper but need complex AI to interpret scenes.

Many AVs use a **fusion** of LiDAR, radar, and vision to improve redundancy and safety.

Urban vs. Highway Autonomy

The complexity of autonomous driving
differs based on the environment:

- **Highways**: Easier due to consistent
  lanes, fewer obstacles, and
  predictable behavior. Tesla's
  Autopilot and GM's Super Cruise
  excel here.

- **Urban Streets**: More
  unpredictable—pedestrians, bikes,
  erratic drivers. Requires advanced
  scene understanding and real-time
  adaptation.

Machine learning models must be
context-aware to handle these variations.
Urban AVs need more powerful computing
and extensive training data.

Challenges and Limitations

Despite the hype, full autonomy remains elusive. Key hurdles include:

1. **Edge Cases**: Rare events like a pedestrian dressed as a bush or an overturned truck.

2. **Weather**: Rain, snow, fog interfere with sensors.

3. **Infrastructure**: Poor road markings, faded signs, unstructured environments.

4. **Ethical Dilemmas**: Who should the car protect in an unavoidable crash?

5. **Public Trust**: Accidents—even if rare—cause public backlash.

6. **Regulations**: Vary by country and state, creating legal uncertainty.

Solving these requires not just better ML models but **collaborative ecosystems** involving governments, urban planners, and citizens.

AV Startups and Innovation Hubs

Beyond tech giants, hundreds of startups are innovating:

- **Aurora**: Building the Aurora Driver platform for multiple vehicle types.

- **Zoox (Amazon)**: Creating a bidirectional vehicle for shared autonomy.

- **Nuro**: Focused on last-mile delivery pods.

- **May Mobility**: Operating autonomous shuttles in university campuses.

- **Pony.ai and AutoX**: Pioneers in the Chinese AV market.

Innovation hubs include:

- **Silicon Valley**: Core of U.S. AV R&D.

- **Detroit**: Traditional auto giants modernizing with AV labs.

- **Munich**: German engineering meets AI.

- **Bangalore**: India's growing AI talent applied to mobility.

Cybersecurity and Safety Protocols

AVs are attractive targets for cyber threats. Security measures include:

- **End-to-end encryption** of sensor data.

- **Secure Over-the-Air (OTA) updates**.

- **Redundant systems** for failsafe operation.

- **Penetration testing** of control modules.

Machine learning also helps detect anomalies and unauthorized behavior in real time.

Safety standards include:

- **ASIL (Automotive Safety Integrity Level)** guidelines for critical functions.

- **ISO 26262** standard for functional safety of electrical/electronic systems.

- **UL 4600** for safety of autonomous products.

Compliance is key to gaining regulatory and consumer trust.

Ethics and Legal Frameworks

With machines making decisions that can affect lives, ethical frameworks are essential. Questions include:

- Should AVs always prioritize passenger safety?

- Who is liable in a crash—developer, owner, or algorithm provider?

- How should AVs handle accidents involving animals or property?

Regulatory bodies are forming advisory panels, and some countries are mandating **AI ethics training** for AV developers. The conversation is evolving.

The Future: What Comes After Autonomy?

Autonomous vehicles will transform industries:

- **Insurance**: Risk models will shift from drivers to manufacturers and algorithms.

- **Real Estate**: Parking demand may decline, freeing urban space.

- **Logistics**: Driverless freight and delivery will slash costs and time.

- **Retail**: Mobile shops and autonomous vending vehicles may emerge.

- **Healthcare**: AVs can transport the elderly or deliver medicine.

We may also see:

- **Modular vehicles**: Swappable interiors for different use cases.

- **Vehicle-as-a-Service (VaaS)**: Subscription models replacing ownership.

- **Smart cities** integrating AVs into traffic systems and energy grids.

Conclusion: Learning to Let Go of the Wheel

Autonomous vehicles, powered by machine learning, are rewriting the rules of mobility. They promise a future of safer roads, greater access, and smarter cities. But that future hinges on solving technological, social, and ethical puzzles.

Machine learning doesn't make AVs perfect—it makes them continually better. Every mile driven, every stop sign recognized, every unexpected event is another lesson learned. We're watching a technology grow, mature, and eventually—drive us into a new era.

In the next chapter, we'll shift focus from the road to the factory—exploring how AI is transforming **vehicle design and manufacturing**, making factories smarter, faster, and more adaptive than ever before.

Chapter 4: AI in Vehicle Design and Manufacturing

The intelligent car begins with an intelligent factory. From the designer's sketchpad to the factory floor, AI is revolutionizing every step of automotive creation.

The automobile is no longer just a mechanical marvel; it is a product of data, simulation, robotics, and intelligence. Behind the sleek silhouette of a modern car lies a symphony of AI-driven decisions—starting from how the vehicle is conceived, to how it's engineered, built, tested, and even how its digital twin evolves in the cloud.

This chapter explores how AI is fundamentally transforming the design and manufacturing processes of the automotive industry. It's not just about building smarter cars—it's about **building cars smarter**.

The End of Traditional Design

For most of the 20th century, vehicle design was a linear, top-down process:

1. Designers sketched ideas manually.

2. Engineers calculated feasibility using CAD tools.

3. Prototypes were built and tested in physical wind tunnels or crash labs.

4. Changes required time-consuming iterations and expensive materials.

While Computer-Aided Design (CAD) and Computer-Aided Engineering (CAE) streamlined some parts, the design process remained slow, rigid, and dependent on human intuition.

With the rise of **Artificial Intelligence**, design becomes:

- **Generative**: AI proposes thousands of variations based on goals.

- **Adaptive**: Designs evolve with real-time feedback from tests.

- **Personalized**: Models can be adjusted for user segments or regions.

- **Simulated**: Entire vehicles can be crash-tested virtually, reducing material waste.

AI-Driven Generative Design

One of the most disruptive technologies in design is **generative design**, powered by AI. Here's how it works:

1. The engineer inputs goals (e.g., weight, strength, cost).

2. Constraints are applied (e.g., material type, safety norms).

3. AI generates thousands of design permutations.

4. The system uses machine learning to select optimal solutions.

5. Human designers refine the best candidates.

Benefits include:

- Lightweighting for better fuel economy or EV range.

- Structural optimization for crash safety.

- Faster time-to-market due to fewer redesign cycles.

Case Example:
General Motors used Autodesk's generative design platform to redesign a seat bracket. The result? A structure 40% lighter and 20% stronger, produced with fewer parts.

AI in Styling and Aerodynamics

Design is not just engineering—it's also **aesthetics** and **aerodynamics**.

AI can:

- Analyze customer preferences and market trends to suggest popular design languages.

- Generate exterior styling options that resonate with specific geographies.

- Simulate airflow digitally, reducing the need for physical wind tunnels.

- Optimize design for both beauty and efficiency.

Tools like **Siemens NX**, **Dassault Systèmes CATIA**, and **Ansys Discovery Live** now integrate AI to support these capabilities.

Digital Twins: Simulating the Vehicle in Real-Time

A **Digital Twin** is a virtual replica of a physical object, continuously updated with real-world data.

For automotive applications, digital twins enable:

- Continuous design feedback during development.

- Virtual crash testing, aerodynamics simulation, and structural analysis.

- Real-time comparison of simulated vs. actual performance in the field.

For example, a digital twin of a car's suspension system can simulate how different driving styles or terrains affect durability—long before a single prototype is built.

Digital twins also extend to the manufacturing environment, enabling virtual commissioning of plants and machinery before physical deployment.

Smart Factories: Industry 4.0 in Motion

AI is the engine of **Industry 4.0**, where manufacturing becomes intelligent, interconnected, and adaptive.

Key components of an AI-powered smart factory include:

- **Industrial IoT (IIoT)**: Sensors on machines collect data in real time.

- **Edge Computing**: AI processes data locally for ultra-fast decision-making.

- **Predictive Maintenance**: Machine learning models detect anomalies before breakdowns occur.

- **Collaborative Robots (Cobots)**: AI-driven robots work alongside humans safely and efficiently.

- **Autonomous Mobile Robots (AMRs)**: Self-driving robots move parts across the plant, optimizing routes based on real-time factory conditions.

AI in Quality Control and Inspection

Defects in manufacturing can cost millions. AI enhances quality control in multiple ways:

- **Computer Vision** inspects parts for cracks, warping, and surface defects faster and more accurately than humans.

- **Deep Learning** identifies subtle patterns in defects to trace root causes.

- **Automated Optical Inspection (AOI)** in electronics and chassis manufacturing ensures reliability.

Case Example:
 BMW uses AI to scan car doors during assembly to detect surface flaws invisible to the human eye. The result is higher quality and reduced rework time.

Supply Chain Optimization with AI

Manufacturing vehicles involves complex global supply chains. AI helps optimize:

- **Demand Forecasting**: Neural networks analyze sales, seasonality, promotions, and external factors.

- **Inventory Management**: AI adjusts inventory levels dynamically to avoid stockouts or overstocking.

- **Supplier Risk Management**: ML models identify high-risk suppliers based on past delays, financial health, and geopolitical events.

Case Example:
Toyota uses AI to detect early signs of supplier disruption (e.g., strikes, weather events) and reroutes procurement or adjusts production schedules proactively.

Human-Robot Collaboration

The rise of **Collaborative Robots (Cobots)** marks a major shift. These AI-driven robots:

- Work safely alongside humans without cages.

- Learn tasks via demonstration (no programming needed).

- Handle precision tasks, reducing ergonomic injuries.

- Can be re-tasked quickly for different models or tasks.

AI ensures cobots can detect human presence, respond to voice commands, and even learn new skills over time.

Real-world application:
Ford uses cobots in engine assembly plants to assist workers in installing heavy or complex components.

Natural Language Interfaces on the Factory Floor

AI-powered assistants are entering the shop floor:

- Workers can interact with machines using **voice commands** or chatbots.

- **AR/VR interfaces** help guide training and repairs.

- **Digital Assistants** pull up specifications, safety procedures, or instructions on demand.

This reduces cognitive load, improves worker productivity, and shortens training time for new recruits.

Additive Manufacturing and AI

3D printing, or **additive manufacturing**, is enhanced with AI:

- ML models suggest optimal geometries and material compositions.

- AI helps auto-correct print anomalies mid-process.

- Real-time sensors in printers adjust parameters like temperature and extrusion flow.

This enables rapid prototyping and even low-volume production of complex components, especially in EVs and motorsport applications.

The Rise of Hyper-Automation

Hyper-automation combines AI, robotics, analytics, and process automation to digitize every aspect of manufacturing.

AI-driven tools now handle:

- **Production scheduling** and re-balancing.

- **Tool calibration** without human intervention.

- **Automated procurement** based on real-time BOM consumption.

It's the leap from traditional automation to full-scale, self-regulating factories.

Energy and Sustainability in the Factory

AI is helping factories go green:

- **Energy Management Systems** optimize power consumption.

- **Thermal mapping** via AI predicts HVAC efficiency.

- **Water recycling systems** adapt based on predicted usage.

- **Carbon tracking** helps companies hit net-zero targets.

As regulations tighten, factories must prove their green credentials—and AI makes it measurable and achievable.

Safety, Ergonomics, and Workforce Wellbeing

AI supports a safer, more human-centric factory:

- **Wearables** with sensors detect fatigue or hazardous postures.

- **AI cameras** monitor worker behavior for unsafe acts.

- **Exoskeletons**, guided by AI, reduce muscular stress.

- **Smart PPE (Personal Protective Equipment)** sends real-time alerts to supervisors.

This technology doesn't just improve safety—it enhances job satisfaction and reduces turnover.

Global Trends and Case Studies

Volkswagen's Smart Production:
Uses AI to analyze over 500 variables per production cycle across its plants worldwide—enabling predictive scheduling and real-time quality assurance.

Hyundai's Meta-Factory Vision:
A full digital twin of its EV factory in Singapore simulates processes, predicts failures, and trains staff via VR.

Tesla's Gigafactory AI:
Optimizes battery cell production using machine vision, predictive analytics, and robotic arms guided by deep learning.

Tata Motors (India):
Implements AI in manufacturing for die-casting optimization, predictive failure modeling, and energy use analytics.

Workforce Transformation

The smart factory needs smart people:

- **Design Engineers** learn to use AI co-pilots for simulations.

- **Line Workers** get reskilled in robotics, data input, and AI dashboards.

- **Plant Managers** become orchestrators of digital ecosystems.

- **AI Specialists** and **Data Scientists** join traditional mechanical teams.

Collaboration between human intuition and AI insights becomes the norm, not the exception.

The Roadblocks

Despite incredible promise, challenges
remain:

- **Data Silos**: Many plants struggle
  with integrating legacy systems.

- **Cybersecurity Risks**: As factories
  go online, vulnerabilities increase.

- **Change Resistance**: Some
  workforces fear AI may replace
  human jobs.

- **High Initial Costs**: Setting up smart
  systems requires capital.

- **Interoperability**: Mismatched
  platforms and protocols can delay
  integration.

Overcoming these requires leadership,
investment, and a culture of lifelong
learning.

Conclusion: From Assembly Lines to Intelligent Lines

AI is doing for manufacturing today what the assembly line did a century ago—**redefining the limits of production**. The difference? Intelligence, flexibility, personalization, and sustainability.

Designers no longer just draw lines—they collaborate with algorithms to shape the future. Factories no longer just assemble—they analyze, adapt, and optimize in real time. And workers no longer just follow commands—they work alongside digital partners.

In the next chapter, we'll explore how AI continues its transformative path—this time in **Predictive Maintenance and Vehicle Diagnostics**, helping vehicles heal themselves before failure strikes.

Chapter 5: Predictive Maintenance and AI Diagnostics

Before a vehicle breaks down, AI already knows why, when, and how to fix it. Welcome to the age of predictive precision.

Gone are the days when vehicle maintenance meant reacting to dashboard warnings or breaking down on the side of the road. In the new world of AI-enhanced mobility, cars don't just report problems—they anticipate them. Predictive maintenance, empowered by artificial intelligence and the Internet of Things (IoT), is revolutionizing how vehicles are monitored, serviced, and kept road-ready.

This chapter explores how AI is transforming diagnostics, reducing downtime, and saving billions for manufacturers, fleet operators, and consumers. Through sensors, machine learning models, and cloud-based analytics, vehicles are becoming proactive partners in their own care.

From Reactive to Predictive: The Maintenance Evolution

Traditional vehicle maintenance strategies have historically fallen into three categories:

1. **Reactive Maintenance**: Fix it when it breaks. The most common and most costly approach.

2. **Preventive Maintenance**: Schedule routine services (oil changes, brake checks) based on time or mileage.

3. **Predictive Maintenance**: Use real-time data to forecast when and what will fail, and act before it happens.

Predictive maintenance combines historical data, real-time sensor input, and AI models to detect anomalies, understand degradation trends, and recommend precise interventions—*just in time*.

Key Technologies Enabling Predictive Maintenance

1. **Telematics Systems**

   o Collect real-time data on engine performance, fuel consumption, GPS location, RPM, braking behavior, and more.

   o Transmit this data to centralized platforms for analysis.

2. **IoT Sensors**

   o Monitor temperature, pressure, vibration, oil quality, battery health, tire pressure, and more.

   o Installed on key components: brakes, powertrain, cooling systems, etc.

3. **Machine Learning Algorithms**

- Identify patterns that precede component failure.

- Predict Remaining Useful Life (RUL) of parts.

- Use clustering and classification to detect outliers or anomalies.

4. **Cloud-Based Analytics**

- Massive computing power for real-time processing and long-term storage.

- Integrates with fleet management systems and service networks.

5. **Edge AI**

- Processes data locally on the vehicle to reduce latency.

- Enables immediate alerts even without internet connectivity.

The AI Diagnostic Process: Step by Step

1. **Data Acquisition**: Sensors gather mechanical, electrical, and environmental data.

2. **Preprocessing**: Noise reduction, normalization, and filtering.

3. **Feature Extraction**: Identifying meaningful data points like vibration frequency spikes.

4. **Model Training**: Historical failure cases used to teach AI what patterns to look for.

5. **Inference**: Real-time data compared to trained models to predict faults.

6. **Action**: Alert sent to driver, mechanic, or cloud dashboard. Service scheduled, part ordered, or fault prevented.

Real-World Applications

1. Engine Health Monitoring
AI can detect micro-vibrations, unusual knock patterns, or exhaust gas anomalies that indicate combustion inefficiencies or valve wear—long before the check engine light turns on.

2. Battery Diagnostics in EVs

- Predicts thermal runaway, cell imbalance, and charging anomalies.

- AI models assess degradation patterns and suggest optimal charging behaviors.

3. Tire and Brake Wear Detection

- AI monitors ABS data, wheel speed variance, and tread sensors.

- Can estimate tread depth and brake pad life precisely.

4. Transmission and Drivetrain Analysis

- Uses vibration sensors and oil quality sensors.

- Detects gear slippage, torque irregularities, and lubrication breakdowns.

Case Study: Tesla's Self-Diagnosing Systems

Tesla's vehicles exemplify AI-powered diagnostics:

- Constant telemetry from every vehicle uploaded to Tesla servers.

- When a fault pattern is detected, Tesla schedules a service appointment before the user even notices.

- In some cases, **software updates fix hardware symptoms**—a failing charging port motor may get remapped to operate differently.

This predictive model reduces service center overload and increases customer satisfaction.

Fleet Operations and Predictive Maintenance

In fleet industries—taxis, delivery, logistics, rental cars—predictive maintenance is mission-critical.

Benefits include:

- **Reduced Downtime**: Vehicles stay operational longer.

- **Lower Costs**: Early intervention avoids catastrophic failures.

- **Optimized Scheduling**: Repairs are planned during low-demand periods.

- **Better Utilization**: Maximized lifespan of expensive assets.

Amazon, **UPS**, **DHL**, and **Uber** all use predictive systems to maintain their growing fleets.

AI in Dealership and Service Networks

Dealerships are also transforming:

- **Diagnostic AI Platforms**:
  Mechanics use tablets that analyze
  real-time vehicle data and
  recommend fixes.

- **Smart Service Advisors**: AI bots
  handle appointments, explain
  issues, and order parts.

- **Inventory Optimization**: AI predicts
  parts demand based on regional
  driving behavior and environmental
  conditions.

Example:
*Toyota's T-Connect and Honda's
Maintenance Minder provide predictive
alerts, connect drivers to the nearest service
center, and sync vehicle history with dealer
systems.*

Predictive Maintenance in Manufacturing

AI diagnostics isn't limited to on-road vehicles—it also plays a vital role in **automotive manufacturing**:

- Detects wear in robotic arms, conveyor motors, and die-casting machinery.

- Prevents unexpected plant shutdowns.

- Balances workloads based on machine health.

- Integrates with ERP and MES platforms to auto-adjust production.

AI Models and Techniques Used

1. **Random Forests**

   - Popular for classifying normal vs. abnormal behavior.

   - Robust to outliers and missing data.

2. **Support Vector Machines (SVM)**

   - Effective in detecting subtle shifts in data.

   - Common in vibration-based failure prediction.

3. **Deep Learning (CNNs, RNNs)**

   - Analyze images from thermal cameras or spectrograms.

   - Sequence-based models for time-series sensor data.

4. **Bayesian Networks**

- Probabilistic reasoning about component interactions.

- Used in complex systems like hybrid powertrains.

5. **Reinforcement Learning**

- Continually adjusts thresholds and alert settings.

- Learns optimal maintenance policies over time.

Predictive Maintenance in Autonomous Vehicles

Autonomous vehicles (AVs) raise the stakes—**they must diagnose themselves**:

- Edge AI constantly monitors vehicle health.

- Predictive algorithms are more aggressive to ensure 100% uptime.

- Some AVs carry **self-repair kits** or direct themselves to service depots.

Waymo, Cruise, and Nuro have invested heavily in AI diagnostics to ensure passenger trust and operational efficiency.

Connected Platforms and Ecosystems

Predictive maintenance thrives on integration:

- **OEM Cloud** (e.g., BMW's CarData, Mercedes Me) collects vehicle data.

- **Third-Party Platforms** (e.g., Uptake, Pitstop, Otonomo) offer plug-and-play predictive insights.

- **Aftermarket Devices**: OBD-II dongles with AI offer diagnostics for older cars.

The ecosystem enables collaboration between drivers, OEMs, dealerships, insurance, and urban authorities.

Challenges in AI Diagnostics

Despite its promise, several challenges exist:

1. **Data Quality and Standardization**

    o   Inconsistent sensor calibration, noisy inputs, and varied driving conditions.

2. **Model Explainability**

    o   Black-box models must be interpretable for regulatory and mechanical validation.

3. **False Positives/Negatives**

    o   Can lead to unnecessary repairs or overlooked issues.

4. **Cybersecurity Risks**

    o   Hackers might spoof diagnostics to disable vehicles or manipulate warranties.

5. Privacy Concerns

- ○ Vehicle owners may be unaware their driving behavior is being continuously logged and analyzed.

Sustainability and Environmental Gains

Predictive maintenance supports sustainability:

- Reduces material waste through timely repairs.

- Extends vehicle and part lifespan.

- Decreases fuel consumption by maintaining optimal performance.

- Supports circular economy with better part recovery planning.

For EVs, especially, predictive battery diagnostics is essential to manage end-of-life disposal and second-life use cases.

Human and AI Collaboration in Repair

AI doesn't replace mechanics—it **empowers** them:

- Junior technicians get decision support from AI platforms.

- AI explains fault trees and repair sequences visually.

- Mechanics become more like system analysts and software troubleshooters.

Training and certification programs now include AI tools—reshaping the service workforce.

Regulatory and Insurance Implications

Governments and insurers are responding:

- Regulatory frameworks now include **vehicle self-diagnostics** and data logging mandates.

- Insurance companies are using diagnostic data for **dynamic risk pricing**.

- Extended warranties are more viable with better predictive insights.

The Future: Self-Healing Vehicles?

Research is already underway into
self-healing technologies:

- Smart materials that auto-repair
  minor cracks.

- AI-driven thermal management that
  reroutes around failing cells.

- Nano-sensors that stimulate
  chemical repairs.

- Software patches that override
  failing firmware modules.

Though early-stage, these advances signal
a future where vehicles truly take care of
themselves.

Conclusion: From Breakdowns to Breakthroughs

Predictive maintenance and AI diagnostics mark a monumental shift—from machines that fail unpredictably to machines that protect their own functionality.

In the AI-driven automotive world, maintenance is no longer an afterthought—it's a **strategic advantage**, a cost saver, and a pillar of safety. Whether in a personal EV, a logistics fleet, or an autonomous robotaxi, AI ensures mobility never stops moving.

In the next chapter, we'll explore how AI is transforming the **automotive supply chain and logistics systems**—from sourcing parts to delivering final products with unprecedented speed and intelligence.

Chapter 6: AI in Supply Chain and Logistics for Automotive

In the age of intelligent mobility, it's not just vehicles that are smart—the journey of every nut, bolt, and battery is optimized by artificial intelligence.

Behind every car that rolls off the production line lies an intricate, global supply chain. From raw materials sourced on one continent to precision parts manufactured on another, the automotive supply chain is a complex web that must function with military precision. In recent years, that web has been stretched, challenged, and redefined by global disruptions. The answer to that complexity and unpredictability? Artificial Intelligence.

This chapter explores how AI is transforming supply chain and logistics operations in the automotive industry—delivering visibility, agility, and resilience like never before. From procurement to shipping, warehouse management to last-mile delivery, AI enables smarter decisions at every link of the chain.

The Unique Complexity of the Automotive Supply Chain

Unlike many industries, the automotive sector relies on **tens of thousands of components** for each vehicle. The supply chain involves:

- **OEMs** (Original Equipment Manufacturers)

- **Tier 1, 2, and 3 suppliers**

- **Contract manufacturers**

- **Distributors and retailers**

- **Raw material providers**

- **Logistics service providers**

A single missing part—from a sensor chip to a seatbelt—can halt an entire assembly line. Add just-in-time manufacturing, narrow inventory margins, and global sourcing into the mix, and you have a system where disruption is both common and costly.

How AI Optimizes Supply Chain Functions

AI enables end-to-end digital transformation by applying predictive, prescriptive, and real-time decision-making tools across the supply chain.

Here's how:

1. **Demand Forecasting**

   o Uses historical sales, seasonality, promotions, economic data, and weather trends.

   o Machine learning improves accuracy by learning from past errors.

   o Detects demand spikes for new EV models or region-specific variants.

2. **Supply Planning**

   o AI balances supply and demand across manufacturing plants.

- Recommends optimal production schedules based on forecast accuracy and inventory levels.

3. **Inventory Management**

  - ML models detect slow-moving inventory or overstocks.

  - Predictive tools adjust safety stock based on market volatility or shipping delays.

4. **Procurement Optimization**

  - AI evaluates supplier performance, price trends, and delivery reliability.

  - Suggests alternative vendors when risks are identified.

5. **Logistics and Routing**

  - Real-time route optimization for inbound and outbound shipments.

  - Adjusts delivery paths based on traffic, weather, and

customs clearance status.

6. **Warehouse Management**

   ○ AI systems predict peak
     times, optimize shelf space,
     and guide robotic picking.

   ○ Reinforcement learning
     dynamically improves layout
     over time.

7. **Risk Management**

   ○ AI anticipates geopolitical,
     environmental, or supplier
     risks.

   ○ Suggests mitigation
     strategies like alternate ports
     or multi-sourcing.

Case Study: BMW's Control Tower

BMW uses a centralized AI-powered control tower to manage its global supply chain:

- Tracks over 30 million parts from 1,800 suppliers daily.

- Predicts supply interruptions using weather feeds, news data, and supplier performance.

- Suggests shipment re-routing and alternative sourcing on the fly.

This system helped BMW respond faster than competitors during semiconductor shortages in 2021–22.

Real-Time Visibility: AI + IoT + Blockchain

AI thrives on data—and IoT (Internet of Things) provides it:

- **Smart sensors** on containers track location, temperature, shock, and tampering.

- **Connected vehicles** provide live updates on part deliveries.

- **Digital twins** replicate warehouses, ports, and even entire supply chains.

Blockchain, when combined with AI, ensures traceability:

- Verifies the authenticity of parts.

- Monitors carbon emissions through the lifecycle.

- Improves accountability in global sourcing.

Together, these technologies enable a **transparent, trustworthy, and traceable supply chain**.

Supplier Relationship Management

AI transforms how automotive companies manage their vendors:

- Analyzes **on-time delivery**, **defect rates**, and **financial risk**.

- Recommends **multi-sourcing** or **nearshoring** strategies.

- Generates **supplier scorecards** updated in real time.

In the EV industry, where battery components must meet strict safety and sustainability standards, AI-driven supplier audits and ESG tracking are becoming mandatory.

Just-In-Time vs. Just-In-Case: AI Balancing Acts

The industry has long followed **Just-In-Time (JIT)** logistics to reduce warehousing costs. But global shocks (like COVID-19, port congestion, and wars) exposed its fragility.

AI helps balance JIT with **Just-In-Case (JIC)** by:

- Modeling disruption scenarios and estimating financial impacts.

- Recommending critical component buffers.

- Suggesting regional hubs or distributed inventories.

Companies are shifting toward **resilient supply chains**, with AI as their compass.

Predictive Shipping and Delivery

AI tools help companies:

- Forecast **estimated time of arrival (ETA)** more accurately.

- Recommend **mode shifts** (air, road, rail, sea) based on urgency and cost.

- Detect **port bottlenecks**, labor strikes, or route closures in advance.

Example:
Volvo Trucks uses AI to predict delays and reschedule deliveries dynamically, increasing delivery accuracy by 30%.

AI in Warehouse Automation

Modern warehouses are **self-optimizing ecosystems**:

- **Computer vision** tracks goods movement and inventory levels.

- **Autonomous robots** sort, pick, and transport parts with precision.

- **AI-driven slotting systems** assign optimal locations for fast-moving items.

- **Digital twins** simulate layouts to reduce travel time and worker fatigue.

Amazon Robotics, now licensing to automotive OEMs, enables 2–3x faster warehouse throughput.

Packaging and Load Optimization

AI algorithms improve efficiency by:

- Designing optimal **packaging dimensions** to minimize space.

- Creating **3D loading plans** for trucks and containers.

- Reducing **fuel use and carbon emissions** by avoiding partial loads.

Even something as simple as packaging can save millions in logistics costs annually.

Vehicle Delivery and Distribution

For OEMs delivering finished vehicles to dealers and customers:

- **AI predicts dealership demand** and recommends regional allocation.

- **Route optimization tools** reduce fleet emissions.

- **Vehicle condition sensors** monitor shock, tilt, or damage during transit.

In direct-to-consumer EV models, like **Tesla** or **Rivian**, AI coordinates home deliveries, reducing dealership dependency.

AI for Returns and Reverse Logistics

Returns—especially in warranty claims and recalls—are complex and expensive.

AI manages:

- **Root cause analysis** to reduce repeat faults.

- **Automated return authorization** and claim verification.

- **Spare parts recovery** and remanufacturing for circular economy compliance.

Predictive analytics reduce warranty costs and improve customer satisfaction.

**Strategic Sourcing and Procurement
Intelligence**

AI platforms can:

- Track global commodity prices
  (steel, lithium, rare earth metals).

- Model the impact of tariffs or
  sanctions on part costs.

- Forecast **currency fluctuations** in
  import-heavy supply chains.

This allows **real-time renegotiation** of
supplier contracts and **early risk
mitigation**.

Resilience Through AI Simulation

Supply chains must prepare for the unexpected.

AI supports **scenario planning**:

- What if a port closes?

- What if a key supplier goes bankrupt?

- What if demand doubles in one region?

Digital twins simulate outcomes and recommend action plans—rerouting, reallocation, alternative vendors.

Sustainability and Green Logistics

AI promotes eco-friendly practices:

- **Optimizes routing** to reduce emissions.

- **Monitors carbon output** across shipments.

- **Suggests modal shifts** to lower-carbon transport.

- **Identifies suppliers** with green certifications.

As regulations like Europe's **Fit for 55** and **CBAM** take effect, AI ensures compliance and reporting accuracy.

Case Study: Toyota's AI Supply Chain in Action

During the 2021 global chip shortage, Toyota's early investments in AI-based risk detection paid off. Their system:

- Identified potential shortages 3–6 months in advance.

- Suggested alternative chip designs and suppliers.

- Rebalanced global production schedules proactively.

Toyota outperformed peers by maintaining higher production continuity during the crisis.

AI + Human Synergy: The Logistics Workforce Reimagined

AI augments logistics professionals:

- **Planners** get instant insights instead of spreadsheets.

- **Warehouse staff** follow AI-optimized picking sequences.

- **Procurement officers** receive negotiation prompts based on market data.

- **Truck drivers** get smart navigation and real-time alerts.

New roles like **supply chain data analyst**, **AI fleet coordinator**, and **logistics simulation architect** are emerging.

Challenges and Ethical Considerations

- **Data Silos**: Integrating legacy ERP with AI is complex.

- **Bias in Algorithms**: AI may favor certain suppliers or regions.

- **Job Displacement**: Automation reduces manual roles.

- **Cybersecurity**: Global logistics systems are increasingly vulnerable to cyberattacks.

- **Global Inequality**: Smaller suppliers may be left out of AI networks.

Mitigating these requires inclusive design, cybersecurity protocols, and ethical sourcing frameworks.

The Road Ahead: Self-Healing Supply Chains

Looking to the future, we'll see:

- **Autonomous delivery vehicles** for parts and finished cars.

- **AI-optimized microfactories** producing vehicles closer to demand.

- **Crowdsourced freight exchanges** powered by real-time AI.

- **Self-rebalancing inventory systems** that learn and adapt to consumption trends.

- **Climate-resilient logistics models** that reroute during natural disasters.

AI will make supply chains not just fast or efficient—but **intelligent, adaptive, and regenerative**.

Conclusion: From Fragility to Fluidity

The automotive supply chain is the nervous system of the entire industry. For decades, it has operated under tight constraints, immense complexity, and high sensitivity to disruption. With AI, this system evolves from reactive to **proactive**, from fragmented to **integrated**, from rigid to **resilient**.

Cars may be the final product—but behind every gear and gadget lies a supply network that thinks, learns, and improves with every shipment.

In the next chapter, we'll look at how AI is transforming **smart mobility and urban transportation systems**—reshaping how vehicles, infrastructure, and people interact in real-time.

Chapter 7: Smart Mobility — AI and Urban Transportation

In the future city, mobility is not about owning a car—it's about access, efficiency, and intelligence. And AI is the traffic controller of it all.

Urban mobility is undergoing a seismic shift. As megacities grow, congestion thickens, pollution rises, and traditional transportation models buckle under pressure, the concept of mobility is being reimagined. No longer confined to private car ownership, mobility today encompasses shared rides, micromobility, mass transit, and autonomous fleets—all seamlessly connected and managed by artificial intelligence.

In this chapter, we examine how AI is transforming urban transportation—building smarter cities, connected vehicles, predictive traffic systems, and more sustainable transit options. From real-time congestion management to AI-powered public transport optimization, this is the operating system of the modern metropolis.

What Is Smart Mobility?

Smart mobility refers to the use of digital technologies—especially AI, IoT, and data analytics—to enhance the efficiency, safety, accessibility, and sustainability of urban transportation systems.

It includes:

- Intelligent traffic systems

- On-demand ride services

- Multimodal journey planning

- Real-time public transit updates

- Autonomous vehicle fleets

- Data-driven infrastructure planning

The ultimate goal: to move people and goods **faster, cheaper, cleaner**, and **smarter**.

The Pain Points of Urban Transport

Cities today face mounting challenges:

- **Congestion**: Urban roads are gridlocked during peak hours.

- **Air Pollution**: Transportation accounts for ~25% of global CO_2 emissions.

- **Inefficiency**: Buses and trains often run empty or off-schedule.

- **Accessibility Gaps**: Many areas remain underserved by reliable transit.

- **Parking Shortages**: Drivers waste time and fuel searching for spots.

Traditional approaches—building more roads or increasing fleet sizes—no longer suffice. A **data-driven, AI-powered mobility model** is the only viable way forward.

AI's Role in Smart Urban Mobility

AI technologies enhance every component of modern transport systems. Here's how:

1. **Traffic Prediction and Management**

   - Machine learning models analyze historical and real-time data.

   - Predict congestion hotspots 30–60 minutes in advance.

   - Adjust signal timings dynamically to reduce delays.

2. **AI-Optimized Public Transit**

   - Predicts passenger demand at specific locations and times.

   - Recommends dynamic bus routing and frequency changes.

- Matches fleet deployment with urban events or weather shifts.

3. **Multimodal Journey Planning**

   - Integrates buses, subways, bike-sharing, taxis, and walking routes.

   - AI suggests optimal combinations based on time, cost, and carbon footprint.

4. **Ridesharing and Demand Prediction**

   - Algorithms match passengers traveling in similar directions.

   - Dynamic pricing and surge detection optimize fleet use.

5. **Autonomous Urban Fleets**

   - AVs handle first- and last-mile transportation.

   - Reduce emissions and free up public space.

Case Study: Singapore's Smart City Mobility Model

Singapore is a global leader in smart mobility:

- AI-based traffic prediction system reduces jams during peak hours.

- Autonomous shuttles operate in industrial parks and campuses.

- Smart traffic lights adjust based on pedestrian volume and emergency vehicles.

- Real-time transit apps combine buses, trains, and bicycles into one route plan.

The result? Efficient, multimodal urban transport with a high satisfaction rate among residents.

Connected Infrastructure: V2X Communication

Vehicle-to-Everything (V2X) enables communication between:

- **Vehicle to Infrastructure (V2I)**: Traffic signals, parking meters, road signs.

- **Vehicle to Vehicle (V2V)**: Prevent collisions and enable platooning.

- **Vehicle to Pedestrian (V2P)**: Alerting cars about nearby walkers or cyclists.

- **Vehicle to Cloud (V2C)**: Updating routes, software, and alerts from central systems.

AI enables interpretation of these data flows in real time, adjusting vehicle behavior, navigation, and traffic control.

AI in Traffic Control Centers

Modern cities deploy **AI-powered control centers**:

- Use CCTV, GPS, sensors, and social media feeds.

- Detect incidents, bottlenecks, and emergencies.

- Activate rerouting strategies and alert emergency services instantly.

- Predict future traffic states and suggest infrastructure adjustments.

Example:
Barcelona's AI platform reduced average commute time by 20% by reallocating bus frequencies and adjusting traffic signals dynamically.

Micromobility: AI Meets Two Wheels

Micromobility—e-scooters, e-bikes, and traditional cycles—is booming in cities. AI plays a pivotal role:

- Predicts usage hotspots to rebalance fleet locations.

- Prevents sidewalk clutter via geofencing and parking analytics.

- Detects unsafe riding behavior or vandalism through computer vision.

- Suggests maintenance schedules based on wear patterns.

Companies like Lime, Bird, and Spin use AI to maximize uptime and user experience.

Smart Parking Solutions

Finding parking is a major urban headache. AI helps by:

- Monitoring parking lot occupancy via cameras and sensors.

- Directing drivers to nearest available spots via apps.

- Implementing **dynamic pricing** based on demand.

- Predicting parking needs near events or construction sites.

Cities like San Francisco, Copenhagen, and Seoul have reduced cruising-for-parking time by 30–40% with smart systems.

AI and the Urban Logistics Puzzle

The rise of e-commerce has overloaded city logistics networks.

AI helps by:

- Predicting delivery volumes by neighborhood and time.

- Optimizing warehouse-to-doorstep routes.

- Coordinating **urban consolidation centers** to reduce freight trips.

- Enabling drone and robot deliveries for last-mile efficiency.

Example:
FedEx uses AI to determine optimal drop-off times in dense areas, improving delivery speed and reducing fuel use.

Smart Mobility and Environmental Sustainability

AI improves environmental outcomes through:

- **Eco-routing**: Directing drivers along fuel-efficient paths.

- **Traffic smoothing**: Reducing idling and stop-go driving.

- **EV Routing and Charging**: Directing drivers to optimal charging stations with minimal wait.

- **Fleet Electrification**: Guiding city agencies on transitioning to electric buses and taxis.

Cities like Oslo and Amsterdam are nearing **zero-emission mobility zones**, enabled by AI-based traffic and fleet management.

Urban Mobility as a Service (MaaS)

MaaS platforms bundle multiple mobility services into one app:

- Book and pay for transit, rideshares, bikes, scooters.

- Use AI to recommend combinations based on user habits.

- Provide real-time updates on delays, congestion, or alternate options.

Whim (Finland), **Moovit (Intel)**, and **Citymapper** lead the MaaS charge, integrating AI with user-centric design.

Data Privacy and Ethics in Urban AI

As AI monitors movement, collects behavioral data, and makes recommendations, privacy becomes a concern:

- Cities must implement **data anonymization** and **user consent** mechanisms.

- **Bias in algorithms** must be addressed to ensure accessibility and fairness.

- Regulations like **GDPR** and **CCPA** apply to mobility data as well.

Transparent governance and public engagement are critical to gaining user trust.

Digital Twins of Cities

AI enables **city-scale simulations**:

- Digital twins model traffic, pollution, and pedestrian flow.

- Urban planners test policy changes—like congestion pricing or bus lane extensions—before implementing them.

- Emergency scenarios (e.g., floods, parades, protests) can be modeled to guide real-time response.

Helsinki and **Shanghai** are among cities deploying digital twins for daily operations and long-term planning.

Challenges in AI-Powered Urban Mobility

- **Fragmented Systems**: Data silos across agencies, operators, and services.

- **Equity Concerns**: AI tools must prioritize underserved communities.

- **Overdependence**: Systems must function during outages or cyberattacks.

- **Public Resistance**: Surveillance fears and data misuse remain hurdles.

- **Funding and Politics**: Infrastructure upgrades and AI systems require sustained investment and cross-party support.

Overcoming these requires integrated policymaking, stakeholder engagement, and ethical AI development.

Future Visions: What Comes Next?

- **Autonomous Public Transport**: Shuttles and buses without drivers.

- **AI-Curated Streets**: Lanes dynamically repurposed for buses, bikes, or delivery bots.

- **Mobility Credits**: AI-driven systems rewarding citizens for low-emission choices.

- **Smart Pavement**: Embedded sensors tracking road wear and weather impact.

- **Urban Aerial Vehicles**: Drones and air taxis managed via AI-driven air traffic control.

Tomorrow's cities will be shaped not just by architects, but by algorithms.

Conclusion: AI—The Traffic Controller of Tomorrow's Cities

Smart mobility is not just a tech trend—it's a necessity for urban survival. With exploding populations and climate concerns, cities must rethink how people and goods move. Artificial Intelligence offers the intelligence, flexibility, and foresight to orchestrate this transformation.

Whether it's a bus arriving on time, a scooter charged and ready, or traffic lights adapting to real-time flow—AI is the invisible conductor of modern urban symphonies.

In the next chapter, we shift our focus to safety and autonomy—exploring **AI-powered safety systems and advanced driver assistance technologies (ADAS)** that are saving lives on the road every day.

Chapter 8: Safety Systems and Driver Assistance Technologies

When machines learn to protect lives, safety becomes proactive—not reactive. Welcome to the AI-driven era of road safety.

Safety has always been central to the automotive mission, from the first seatbelt to the crumple zone and airbag. But today, safety is no longer a passive set of features triggered during accidents. It is becoming an intelligent, anticipatory system driven by Artificial Intelligence. Vehicles now observe, analyze, and intervene—often before the driver is even aware of a potential hazard.

This chapter dives deep into how AI is transforming road safety through **Advanced Driver Assistance Systems (ADAS)** and intelligent safety features that are reducing fatalities, improving driver awareness, and paving the way for full autonomy.

The Scope of Road Safety Challenges

Despite advances in automotive design and traffic laws, road accidents continue to claim **over 1.3 million lives annually**, according to the World Health Organization. Key causes include:

- Human error (drowsiness, distraction, speeding)

- Poor visibility

- Weather conditions

- Blind spots and poor situational awareness

- Delayed response times

AI doesn't just improve visibility or automate braking—it creates a **360-degree situational awareness layer**, processing millions of data points in real-time to keep all road users safer.

What is ADAS?

Advanced Driver Assistance Systems (ADAS) are technologies that assist drivers in driving and parking functions. These systems use AI, sensors, and cameras to detect the environment around the vehicle and help prevent collisions.

ADAS functions fall into three categories:

1. **Warning Systems**: Alert drivers of potential danger.

2. **Assistance Systems**: Help control the vehicle in certain scenarios.

3. **Control Systems**: Take over specific driving functions to avoid incidents.

Examples include:

- Adaptive Cruise Control (ACC)

- Lane Departure Warning (LDW)

- Automatic Emergency Braking (AEB)

- Blind Spot Detection (BSD)

- Traffic Sign Recognition (TSR)

- Pedestrian and Cyclist Detection

Each of these features requires advanced perception, interpretation, and action—powered by AI models trained on millions of road scenarios.

The AI Toolbox for Safety

AI enables safety systems by powering:

1. **Computer Vision**

    o Detects lanes, pedestrians, vehicles, and signs.

    o Trained using convolutional neural networks (CNNs).

2. **Sensor Fusion Algorithms**

    o Combine inputs from radar, LiDAR, ultrasonic, and camera data.

    o Reduce error margins and improve object detection in complex environments.

3. **Machine Learning Classifiers**

    o Categorize objects and scenarios (e.g., pedestrian about to cross vs. stationary).

- Enable probabilistic reasoning about threats.

4. **Predictive Analytics**

   - Anticipate collisions based on trajectory and speed.

   - Identify driver drowsiness or distraction.

5. **Reinforcement Learning**

   - Optimize system response in dynamic conditions through simulations.

Case Study: Volvo and Vision Zero

Volvo's commitment to **Vision Zero**—no deaths or serious injuries in their vehicles—has been bolstered by AI:

- Pedestrian detection even at night or in fog.

- City Safety suite automatically brakes when detecting cyclists or sudden lane intrusions.

- AI-enhanced cameras differentiate between humans, animals, and objects.

The result? A massive drop in rear-end collisions and pedestrian injuries across Volvo's global fleet.

In-Vehicle Monitoring Systems (IVMS)

AI doesn't just look outward—it also monitors inside the cabin:

- **Driver Monitoring Systems (DMS)** use cameras to detect drowsiness, distraction, and gaze direction.

- AI can recommend breaks, reduce speed, or even bring the vehicle to a safe stop.

- Facial recognition prevents vehicle theft or unauthorized use.

As regulation increases (e.g., EU's General Safety Regulation 2024), DMS will become mandatory—and AI will be its core.

Adaptive and Predictive Systems

Modern safety systems are no longer
rule-based—they are adaptive.

- **Adaptive Cruise Control (ACC)**
  maintains safe distance in traffic.

- **Predictive Forward Collision
  Systems** anticipate merging
  vehicles or pedestrians from
  occluded areas.

- **AI Brake Assist** analyzes speed,
  object distance, and road conditions
  to determine brake force.

AI also adjusts behavior to driver
tendencies, environmental context, and
vehicle state.

Edge AI: Speed Matters in Safety

Latency can mean the difference between life and death.

- AI models for ADAS run on **edge devices** within the car.

- Specialized chips like **NVIDIA DRIVE, Mobileye EyeQ**, and **Qualcomm Snapdragon Ride** ensure real-time decision-making.

- Edge AI avoids delays from cloud processing, ensuring instant response.

Vehicle-to-Everything (V2X) for Safety

AI also processes external inputs via V2X:

- **V2I**: Detect red light runners or slippery roads via smart signals.

- **V2V**: Warn nearby vehicles about sudden braking or collision threats.

- **V2P**: Alert vehicle when a pedestrian is crossing unexpectedly.

These systems are crucial for complex intersections, school zones, or dense urban areas.

Emergency Maneuver Assistance

When collision is imminent:

- **Automatic Emergency Steering** can swerve the vehicle while ensuring stability.

- **Intersection Assistance** prevents left-turn collisions.

- **Roll-Over Prevention** uses gyroscopic data to apply brakes and stabilize.

AI models analyze hundreds of variables per second to execute the safest action.

Weather and Low-Light Adaptation

AI extends safety where human senses falter:

- Thermal cameras detect heat signatures in fog, smoke, or darkness.

- Radar functions in heavy rain or snow.

- AI compensates for glare, sun angles, and night blindness.

This improves safety in rural, high-speed, or unpredictable environments.

Integration with Autonomous Driving

All ADAS functions are foundational for autonomy:

- Level 2–3 systems handle partial self-driving with human oversight.

- Higher levels (L4–L5) combine all ADAS into a unified AI stack.

Companies like **Waymo**, **Tesla**, and **Cruise** rely on these systems as building blocks for autonomy.

Safety Ratings and AI's Influence

Safety organizations like **Euro NCAP, IIHS**, and **NHTSA** now include ADAS in ratings:

- Points awarded for AEB, LDW, BSD, and pedestrian protection.

- AI-enhanced systems improve crash avoidance scores.

OEMs increasingly use AI performance to market vehicle safety.

Insurance and Risk Scoring

AI-powered safety systems impact insurance:

- Usage-Based Insurance (UBI) uses real-time data to adjust premiums.

- Insurers offer discounts for vehicles with AI-enabled ADAS.

- Post-accident data helps reconstruct incidents and determine liability.

In the future, AI may also detect fraud by analyzing crash patterns and behaviors.

AI Safety Standards and Regulations

Standardization is critical:

- **ISO 26262**: Functional safety in automotive electronics.

- **UNECE WP.29**: Cybersecurity and software update regulations.

- **ASIL Ratings**: Risk levels for safety-critical systems.

- **AI Act (EU)** and **NHTSA guidelines** for transparency and testing.

OEMs must ensure AI systems are not just effective—but **accountable, explainable, and certified**.

AI-Powered Safety in Emerging Markets

Cost-effective safety is critical in developing regions:

- AI systems now integrated in vehicles under $20,000.

- Aftermarket retrofits offer ADAS kits with cameras and OBD-II integrations.

- NGOs partner with tech firms to deploy AI safety buses and motorcycles.

AI democratizes safety—saving lives regardless of income level.

Ethics in AI Safety Systems

Ethical design must address:

- **Decision-making priorities** in multi-collision scenarios.

- **Bias in training data** affecting recognition of minorities or vulnerable users.

- **Transparency** in how AI arrives at safety decisions.

- **Consent** for in-cabin monitoring and data storage.

Multistakeholder governance is needed to ensure safety without surveillance overreach.

AI Beyond the Car: Infrastructure Safety

Smart safety extends to:

- **Intelligent crosswalks** that signal vehicles when pedestrians are detected.

- **AI traffic cameras** that identify rule violations and reroute traffic.

- **Emergency vehicle prioritization** using smart signals.

- **Road wear detection** and pothole mapping via crowd-sourced AI.

These systems reduce accident risk even before drivers or cars are involved.

The Future of AI Safety Systems

The next wave of safety includes:

- **Emotion AI**: Detect road rage, anxiety, or impaired cognition.

- **Haptic Feedback AI**: Steering wheel and seat vibrations for warnings.

- **360° Danger Simulation**: AI models simulate 3D scenarios and provide audio cues.

- **Digital Co-Pilots**: Conversational AI that helps during complex situations.

Combined, these systems shift from **warning drivers** to **assisting drivers**—and eventually, to **replacing drivers** in risk scenarios.

Conclusion: AI as the Guardian Angel of Mobility

AI is revolutionizing safety by turning passive systems into proactive guardians. It sees further, reacts faster, and never gets tired. From detecting a cyclist in the dark to gently nudging a distracted driver back on course, AI saves lives—not through brute force, but through intelligent foresight.

The result is a world where every journey becomes safer—not just for the driver, but for everyone sharing the road.

In the next chapter, we'll examine how AI is powering **sustainability and innovation in the automotive sector**, helping the industry cut emissions, adopt circular economy models, and meet the climate goals of the 21st century.

Chapter 9: AI and Sustainable Automotive Innovation

In the age of climate urgency, AI is the steering wheel of sustainability—guiding the automotive world toward zero emissions, circular economies, and a greener future.

The automotive industry, once emblematic of industrial prowess and freedom, is today under immense pressure to transform—not only to meet customer demand and innovation benchmarks but also to address its environmental footprint. The planet is warming, cities are choking with smog, and fossil fuel reliance is no longer viable. Against this backdrop, Artificial Intelligence emerges not just as a tool for efficiency, but as a compass for **sustainable innovation**.

This chapter explores how AI is accelerating the automotive sector's transition to sustainability—reshaping how vehicles are designed, manufactured, driven, and retired, while aligning the industry with the global pursuit of net-zero emissions.

The Urgency of Change: Automotive and the Climate Crisis

Transportation contributes nearly **25% of global CO_2 emissions**, with passenger vehicles and freight leading the charge. Key sustainability challenges include:

- **Fuel-based emissions** from internal combustion engines.

- **Resource-heavy manufacturing**, especially for EV batteries.

- **Waste and pollution** from retired vehicles and parts.

- **Inefficient supply chains** and long-distance logistics.

Governments, consumers, and regulators are demanding cleaner alternatives. The **Paris Agreement, COP26 goals**, and **2030/2050 Net-Zero Targets** are not optional—they're existential mandates.

AI as the Brain of Sustainability

AI enables sustainability across five major pillars:

1. **Design Optimization**

2. **Energy Efficiency**

3. **Circular Economy and Recycling**

4. **Sustainable Supply Chains**

5. **Consumer Behavior and Smart Mobility**

Let's explore each in depth.

1. AI in Eco-Design and Lightweighting

Designing a sustainable vehicle begins with
material and structural intelligence:

- **Generative Design**: AI creates
  ultra-lightweight structures that
  maintain strength while reducing
  material usage. Less weight means
  better fuel efficiency or EV range.

- **Material Science AI**: Identifies
  alternative materials (e.g., recycled
  composites, plant-based polymers)
  with lower carbon footprints.

- **Lifecycle Assessment (LCA)**: AI
  calculates cradle-to-grave emissions
  of design choices, enabling greener
  trade-offs in early stages.

Case Example:
*BMW's i Vision Circular is a vehicle
designed with AI-optimized components for
full recyclability and zero emissions, using
secondary aluminum and bio-based
materials.*

2. Sustainable Manufacturing Powered by AI

Factories are massive energy consumers and waste generators. AI improves:

- **Energy Optimization**: Monitors and reduces HVAC, lighting, and machinery energy use.

- **Smart Water Use**: AI models manage water recycling systems and detect leaks.

- **Scrap Reduction**: Predicts material defects or overuse before they occur.

- **Emission Mapping**: Real-time CO_2 tracking per production line.

Example:
Volkswagen's Zwickau EV plant uses AI to cut 30% of energy consumption per vehicle, integrating solar energy forecasts to schedule operations efficiently.

3. Battery Innovation and Lifecycle Intelligence

Electric Vehicles are only as green as their batteries. AI helps at every stage:

- **Battery Chemistry Modeling**: Identifies new low-impact materials (e.g., sodium-ion, solid-state) using ML simulations.

- **Charging Optimization**: AI balances fast charging with thermal safety and longevity.

- **Battery Health Monitoring**: Extends lifespan by predicting and preventing degradation.

- **Second-Life Planning**: Determines when EV batteries can be reused in stationary storage before recycling.

Circular battery ecosystems, guided by AI, reduce mining demands and environmental impact.

4. The Circular Economy: AI for Reuse and Recycling

The linear model of build-use-dispose is obsolete. AI enables a **circular economy**:

- **Parts Recovery Forecasting**: Predicts which components can be salvaged post-use.

- **Reverse Logistics**: AI plans the most sustainable routes for part returns or recycling.

- **Smart Dismantling**: Computer vision guides robotic arms to extract reusable modules.

- **Material Sorting**: AI-powered sensors distinguish aluminum from steel, or plastics by polymer type.

Example:
Renault's Refactory in France uses AI to refurbish, remanufacture, and recycle vehicles—adding decades to their usable life.

5. Green Supply Chains and Ethical Sourcing

AI cleans up supply chains:

- **Carbon Tracking**: Measures Scope 1, 2, and 3 emissions across the chain.

- **Route Optimization**: Chooses the lowest-emission paths for freight.

- **Supplier Scoring**: Ranks vendors based on ESG (Environmental, Social, Governance) metrics.

- **Regulatory Compliance**: Automates reporting for REACH, RoHS, and green taxonomies.

AI also flags **conflict minerals**, unethical labor practices, and high-risk zones—helping OEMs source with conscience.

6. Smarter Driving = Greener Driving

Once on the road, AI optimizes energy use:

- **Eco-Routing**: Chooses paths that minimize fuel or battery use.

- **Driving Behavior Coaching**: Recommends smoother acceleration, speed limits, or braking.

- **Real-Time Climate Control Tuning**: Adjusts AC or heating for minimal power draw.

- **Dynamic Tire Pressure Monitoring**: Improves mileage and reduces tire wear.

Example:
Hyundai's GreenZone Drive Mode automatically switches to electric mode in school zones or dense areas based on AI geofencing.

7. AI in Urban Sustainability and Policy Planning

Beyond individual vehicles, AI supports citywide sustainability:

- **EV Charging Infrastructure Planning**: Identifies optimal station locations based on usage patterns.

- **Emissions Zoning**: Suggests low-emission zones and tracks compliance.

- **Shared Mobility Modeling**: Predicts benefits of ride pooling or autonomous shuttles.

- **Public Transit Greening**: Optimizes electric bus routes and schedules.

Cities like **Oslo**, **Beijing**, and **Los Angeles** use AI to reduce vehicular emissions while improving mobility access.

8. Environmental Footprint Calculators for Consumers

AI helps consumers make greener choices:

- **Vehicle Configurators**: Estimate CO_2 savings between petrol, hybrid, and EV models.

- **In-App Carbon Trackers**: Show users their monthly emissions and savings.

- **Gamification**: Rewards low-carbon behaviors like carpooling or smart charging.

Case Example:
Tesla's "Energy Impact Card" and BMW's "My BMW" app use AI to help drivers visualize their impact and improve over time.

9. AI and Alternative Fuels

AI helps accelerate non-battery alternatives:

- **Hydrogen Fuel Cell Optimization**

    - Monitors pressure, flow rate, and heat generation in real-time.

    - Predicts stack failure and recommends maintenance.

- **Biofuel Efficiency Mapping**

    - Tracks engine performance on blends like ethanol or biodiesel.

    - AI adapts combustion parameters dynamically.

AI expands the options for regions where EVs are less viable due to infrastructure gaps.

10. Measuring and Reporting with AI

Sustainability is not just about action—it's about **measurement and accountability**:

- **Automated ESG Reports**: AI generates compliant environmental disclosures.

- **Sustainability Dashboards**: Offer real-time insights across operations.

- **Scenario Simulations**: Predict outcomes of switching to new materials, processes, or fleets.

These tools help companies comply with green regulations while maintaining transparency for investors and customers.

Challenges and Limitations

Despite its promise, AI for sustainability faces barriers:

- **Data Fragmentation**: Inconsistent or incomplete data across the value chain.

- **Model Bias**: Over-optimization of one metric (e.g., CO_2) at the cost of others (e.g., water use).

- **Cost of Implementation**: High initial investments in sensors, compute power, and training.

- **Ethical Trade-offs**: Data collection vs. privacy, automation vs. jobs.

Sustainable AI must be **holistic, explainable, and inclusive**.

Future Trends

Looking ahead, AI will further evolve automotive sustainability through:

- **Climate-Responsive Design**: Vehicles that adapt materials or features based on location's weather risk.

- **Dynamic Carbon Offsetting**: Real-time purchase of carbon credits linked to trip emissions.

- **Hyperlocal Circularity**: Regional microfactories recycling vehicles into local fleets.

- **AI Carbon Tutors**: Personal AI guides to help consumers and businesses lower their transport emissions.

Conclusion: AI as the Engine of Green Mobility

Sustainability in the automotive world is no longer a luxury—it is an imperative. And AI is the core enabler of this transformation. From raw materials to road miles, retirement to reuse, AI makes every step **smarter, cleaner, and more responsible**.

The automotive industry is driving into a future where innovation and responsibility share the same lane—and AI is at the wheel.

In the final chapter, we'll reflect on **the road ahead**—exploring policies, ethics, and the human-AI relationship that will shape the future of cars, cities, and civilization itself.

Chapter 10: The Road Ahead — Policy, Ethics, and the Future

As technology accelerates, society must decide where the road leads. In the AI-powered automotive era, it's not just machines we must teach to drive—it's ourselves we must guide with foresight, ethics, and responsibility.

The integration of AI into the automotive industry has reshaped how vehicles are built, driven, and maintained. But the implications of this transformation go far beyond engineering. As cars evolve from tools of mobility into intelligent, autonomous entities, new questions arise—questions about policy, legal frameworks, human trust, accountability, surveillance, and the kind of future we want to create.

This final chapter of *AI in Automotive Industry* explores the **ethical, regulatory, geopolitical, and philosophical dimensions** of AI-powered mobility. It charts the road ahead—one that is as much about values as it is about vehicles.

The Tension Between Innovation and Regulation

AI's potential to improve road safety, reduce emissions, and revolutionize logistics is clear. But that potential often moves faster than the policies meant to govern it.

Key regulatory challenges include:

- **Lagging Legislation**: Laws governing autonomous vehicles vary wildly between countries and even states.

- **Undefined Liability**: Who is responsible in a crash involving an AI-driven vehicle—the developer, the OEM, or the driver?

- **Cross-border Consistency**: Autonomous vehicles may cross borders, but their regulatory frameworks do not.

- **Data Ownership and Consent**: Who owns driving data? The driver, the carmaker, or the insurer?

Governments must build **agile regulatory ecosystems**—flexible enough to foster innovation, yet robust enough to protect the public.

Global Regulatory Landscape

Let's look at how different regions are responding:

United States:

- Regulation is mostly at the state level.

- The NHTSA provides voluntary guidance on AV safety.

- California leads with AV testing permits and transparency requirements.

European Union:

- The **EU AI Act** introduces risk-based classification for AI systems.

- UNECE regulations mandate cybersecurity and software update protocols.

- ADAS features are being made mandatory under the GSR 2024.

China:

- Leading in AV infrastructure deployment.

- Government-backed companies like Baidu and Pony.ai are trialing robo-taxis.

- Emphasis on data localization and vehicle-to-infrastructure integration.

India, Brazil, and Africa:

- Early-stage frameworks.

- Focus on low-cost AI retrofits for safety and traffic optimization.

- Significant potential for AI leapfrogging in urban planning.

A unified framework, akin to the **ICAO for aviation**, may be needed for global vehicle autonomy standards.

Ethics in AI-Driven Mobility

AI introduces new ethical dilemmas:

1. **Algorithmic Decision-Making**

   - Should a car prioritize the driver or a pedestrian in a crash scenario?

   - What values are embedded in these decisions—and whose values are they?

2. **Bias and Inclusion**

   - AI systems trained predominantly on Western roads may misinterpret environments in developing nations.

   - Facial recognition systems can fail to detect non-white faces with equal accuracy—raising safety and fairness concerns.

3. **Surveillance and Privacy**

   ○ In-cabin monitoring and V2X
     systems collect sensitive
     data.

   ○ Can this data be used for
     advertising, policing, or
     insurance scoring without
     consent?

4. **Job Displacement**

   ○ Autonomous freight and
     robotaxis may displace
     millions of drivers.

   ○ What obligations do we have
     to upskill and reskill affected
     workers?

These questions demand inclusive
dialogue—not just among engineers and
policymakers, but with citizens, ethicists,
and human rights advocates.

Public Trust and Social Acceptance

Technology alone does not guarantee adoption. Trust is critical.

Factors that influence public acceptance:

- **Transparency**: Can the AI explain its actions? Was its training dataset disclosed?

- **Performance**: Does the system perform reliably in diverse weather and environments?

- **Responsiveness**: Are software updates quick and effective after a safety event?

- **Equity**: Are these features available in affordable vehicles, or just luxury models?

Building trust will require **transparency**, **education**, and **accountability** mechanisms.

Insurance, Risk, and Financial Models

AI changes how risk is calculated:

- Traditional insurance assumes driver-centric risk. Autonomous vehicles shift that to OEMs and software vendors.

- New policies may be **usage-based**, **mileage-based**, or **behavior-based**.

- Post-crash data reconstruction (black box data) will be essential to resolve liability.

Insurers must partner with automakers and regulators to design **next-gen risk models**.

AI Governance in the Automotive Sector

Forward-looking companies are establishing **AI governance boards** with oversight on:

- Model fairness

- Data sourcing and annotation

- Explainability audits

- Post-deployment monitoring

AI governance frameworks—modeled on those in healthcare or finance—will become essential as automotive AI matures.

Cybersecurity and AI Integrity

AI makes vehicles smarter—but also more hackable.

Key security measures include:

- **Zero-Trust Architectures**: No internal system is assumed safe.

- **OTA Verification**: Encrypted, authenticated software updates.

- **Anomaly Detection**: AI systems to detect manipulation or rogue commands.

- **Secure V2X Protocols**: Ensuring communication integrity between vehicles and infrastructure.

Governments may mandate **cybersecurity certifications**, just as crash tests are mandated today.

Autonomous Vehicles and Urban Planning

AVs will reshape the physical form of cities:

- **Reduced Parking Demand**: AVs can self-park or operate continuously.

- **Smarter Roads**: AV lanes, dynamic tolling, and automated traffic control.

- **Reclaiming Space**: Parking lots repurposed for housing, parks, or commerce.

- **Decentralized Mobility**: Fleets and micro-hubs may replace monolithic depots.

Urban planners must collaborate with AV developers to avoid replicating past car-centric mistakes.

Human-AI Collaboration in the Driving Experience

AI will not completely replace the driver for many years. The interim will be defined by **collaboration**:

- **Shared Control**: Driver and AI co-pilot the vehicle (e.g., Tesla's Autopilot).

- **Driver Coaching**: AI provides gentle nudges to improve safety.

- **Contextual Handover**: Clear communication when AI needs the driver to resume control.

- **Human-Centric Design**: Interfaces that reduce distraction and cognitive load.

Human-AI interaction must be intuitive, seamless, and fail-safe.

Cultural Shifts in Mobility Behavior

AI is changing not just how we drive, but **why and whether** we drive:

- **Mobility as a Service (MaaS)**: People prioritize access over ownership.

- **Shared Fleets**: Reduce total vehicles per capita.

- **Environmental Awareness**: AI informs users of their carbon impact in real-time.

- **Digital Mobility Twins**: Individuals may have AI avatars optimizing their mobility schedule for speed, cost, or emissions.

A shift from **individualism to interdependence** is underway in transportation culture.

Future Scenarios: 2035 and Beyond

Scenario 1: Autonomous Cities

- Full AV integration.

- AI-managed multimodal traffic.

- Zero-emission zones.

- AI replacing traffic police, parking enforcement, and even urban planning.

Scenario 2: AI Inequality

- Advanced AI safety systems only in luxury vehicles.

- Insurance penalizes those without smart cars.

- Digital divide deepens.

Scenario 3: Balanced Human-Machine Mobility

- Shared control models.

- AI as augmentation, not replacement.

- Strong public-private collaboration.

Which future emerges depends on the choices we make now.

AI for Good: The Broader Impact

Beyond driving, AI in automotive can aid:

- **Disaster Relief**: Autonomous vehicles delivering aid in dangerous zones.

- **Accessibility**: Mobility for elderly and disabled populations.

- **Environmental Stewardship**: AI fleet optimization for wildlife corridors and air quality.

- **Global Development**: Smart minibuses in underserved rural regions.

When designed inclusively, automotive AI becomes a force for global equity.

The Moral of the Machine

In this journey through the AI-powered automotive revolution, we've seen machines become:

- **Learners** (machine learning)

- **Observers** (computer vision)

- **Planners** (path optimization)

- **Guardians** (safety systems)

- **Negotiators** (urban traffic systems)

- **Stewards** (sustainability models)

The question now is not just "Can we build it?" but **"Should we?"** and **"For whom?"**

The future of transportation is not just about intelligent vehicles—it's about wise societies.

Conclusion: The Road Ahead

AI is transforming every bolt, line of code, and second behind the wheel. But as we build more intelligent cars, we must ensure we also build:

- **Just policies**

- **Fair algorithms**

- **Transparent systems**

- **Empowered citizens**

The road ahead is filled with potential. It is also filled with forks, curves, and crossroads. With AI as our engine, and ethics as our compass, we can choose a path that leads not just to faster, smarter, cleaner mobility—but to a better, more human future.

Conclusion

From horsepower to brainpower, the automotive world has come a long way.

As we bring this journey to a close, one thing is clear: **AI is not simply enhancing the automotive industry—it is redefining it.**

We have explored how artificial intelligence now drives innovation in every area of the vehicle lifecycle—from concept design to predictive maintenance, from connected infrastructure to carbon-neutral production lines. Vehicles are no longer isolated machines; they are intelligent nodes in a vast ecosystem of mobility.

But technology, no matter how advanced, is still shaped by human intention. The choices we make about data privacy, sustainability, access, and regulation will determine whether AI in automotive becomes a tool of empowerment or exclusion.

The future is not fully autonomous—it's **co-created**. By developers, policymakers, cities, businesses, and citizens. This book has given you a map; now it's up to you to help drive the journey.

The road ahead is open. Let's make it wise.

Index

A
ADAS – 4, 7, 8
Adaptive Cruise Control – 8
AI Act (EU) – 10
Autonomous Vehicles – 3, 4, 7, 10

B
Battery Lifecycle – 5, 9
Blockchain – 6
Blind Spot Detection – 8

C
Circular Economy – 6, 9
Computer Vision – 3, 8
Cybersecurity – 5, 10

D
Data Privacy – 7, 10
Digital Twin – 2, 6, 9
Driver Monitoring – 5, 8

E
Edge AI – 4, 5, 8
Electric Vehicles – 2, 3, 5, 9
Ethics in AI – 10

F
Fleet Management – 5, 6
Fuel Efficiency – 1, 3, 9

Glossary

ADAS (Advanced Driver Assistance Systems): A suite of safety features that assist the driver using sensors, AI, and machine learning.

AI (Artificial Intelligence): The simulation of human intelligence by machines, enabling learning, reasoning, and adaptation.

Autonomous Vehicle (AV): A vehicle capable of sensing its environment and navigating without human input.

Computer Vision: A field of AI that enables machines to interpret and process visual data from the world.

Digital Twin: A virtual replica of a physical product or process, used to simulate, monitor, and optimize real-world performance.

Edge AI: Running AI algorithms directly on devices (e.g., vehicles) without relying on cloud computing for faster decision-making.

Generative Design: AI-driven process that creates multiple design alternatives based on specified constraints and goals.

IoT (Internet of Things): A network of interconnected devices that collect and exchange data, widely used in vehicles and factories.

LiDAR (Light Detection and Ranging): A remote sensing method that uses laser light to measure distances and create high-resolution maps.

MaaS (Mobility as a Service): A model where users access transportation through digital platforms combining public and private services.

Machine Learning (ML): A subset of AI where systems improve over time by learning from data.

Predictive Maintenance: The use of data and AI to predict when a vehicle or part will fail, enabling proactive repair and reducing downtime.

Reinforcement Learning: A type of machine learning where an agent learns to make decisions by interacting with its environment and receiving feedback.

Sustainability: Practices that reduce environmental impact, conserve resources, and support long-term ecological balance.

V2X (Vehicle-to-Everything): Communication between vehicles and external systems like infrastructure, other vehicles, and pedestrians.